BOA CONSTRICTORS

WEIRD PETS

Lynn M. Stone

Rourke Publishing LLC
Vero Beach, Florida 32964

www.rourkepublishing.com

PHOTO CREDITS:
All photos © Lynn M. Stone

EDITORIAL SERVICES:
Pamela Schroeder

Library of Congress Cataloging-in-Publication Data

Stone, Lynn M.
    Boa Constrictors / Lynn M. Stone
        p. cm—(Weird Pets)
    ISBN 1-58952-036-X
    1.Boa constrictors as pets—Juvenile literature [1. Boa constrictors
as pets. 2. Snakes as pets. 3. Pets.] I. Title.

SF459.S5 S76 2001
639.3'967—dc21   00-054287

Printed in the USA

TABLE OF CONTENTS

BOA CONSTRICTORS

Could you like a pet that wasn't warm and cuddly? People who keep boa **constrictors** do.

Boa constrictors are snakes. They're cool when you touch them, and they are not cuddly.

Boas are unusual pets. However, they are one of the most common snakes in **captivity**. In fact, many boa owners raise their own boa babies. Today most boas being sold as pets were raised in captivity.

Boas learn to feel safe if they're held carefully and often.

Many **species**, or kinds, of boas have become rare in the wild. The boas people usually keep as pets are species from Central or South America. Many of these are called red-tailed or Central American boas.

Boas are the best known kind of constrictor. Constrictors are snakes that kill **prey** by wrapping their bodies around it. A boa's favorite prey is a rat or mouse.

Young people should learn how to handle boas from adults who know the snakes.

The loops of a boa's body are **coils**. The coils squeeze, or constrict, the prey. A boa doesn't crush its prey. The prey dies because the snake's tight coils don't let it breathe. After killing its prey, a boa eats it whole, headfirst. Captive boas are often given dead prey to eat.

Other well-known constrictors are rat snakes and pythons. Pythons are close cousins of boas. One of the few differences between them is that pythons lay eggs. Boas have live babies.

Before eating a rat, a boa kills it with its body coils.

Boas are famous for being huge. Some of them are. At least one boa was more than 18 feet (5.5 meters) long! Most adult boas are 9 to 12 feet (2.7 to 3.7 m) long.

Different boas are different sizes. The word *boa* is used for about 50 different species. Some, like the rubber boa of western North America, are less than 3 feet (1 m) in length.

This Columbia red-tailed boa has been taken from its cage for exercise.

With good care, boas can live at least 40 years in captivity.

A boa's jaws are flexible so it can easily grab and swallow large prey.

BOA CONSTRICTORS: PET FRIENDLY?

Snake owners like boas for many reasons. Adult boas are calm and easy to handle. Some captive snakes are too dangerous to have as pets.

Some snakes won't eat in captivity. Their owners must force them to eat to keep them alive. Boa constrictors, however, like all animals, love to eat. That makes the owner's job easier.

A boa's eyesight is poor, but its forked tongue helps it locate warm prey.

Boas are colorful. They come in many colors and patterns. Some pet boas have colors that you would never see in the wild. Boa **breeders** help create them. They choose which boas should be mothers and fathers. The breeders' choices have made some very unusual boa colors, even pure white.

This Columbia red-tailed boa is a tan color not likely to be found in wild boas.

A boa isn't the right pet for everyone. Young boas have nasty tempers and may bite. A boa's bite isn't poisonous. However, a snake bite is never fun. Most boas become tame if they are held often.

Boas can become long, heavy snakes. Some people don't want to care for such a large animal. In some places it is even against the law to keep a large snake.

Know your town's laws! Big boas like this Columbia red-tailed cannot be kept as a pet in some places.

CARING FOR A BOA CONSTRICTOR

No one should keep a boa until they find out how to care for it. Several books and on-line sources tell about boa care.

Boas don't move around much. They can live calmly in a cage. But, they need a few things to stay healthy. They need a dish of water to soak in. The air around them can't be too hot or too cold. They also need a healthy diet of prey. As a boa grows in size, so should the size of its prey.

With adults nearby, a 5-year-old boy handles a Columbia red-tailed boa almost twice as long as he is.

FINDING A BOA CONSTRICTOR

You can buy boas at many pet shops. You can also find them on-line and through **reptile** clubs.

Prices for boas depend upon the snake's size, species, and color. Some colors are rare. Those boas may cost thousands of dollars.

No one should buy a thin or hot-tempered boa.

GLOSSARY

breeder (BREED er) — a person who raises a kind of animal to sell to other people

captivity (kap TIV eh tee) — being kept by people in a cage, pen, or barn, not in the wild

coil (KOYL) — a loop of a snake's body

constrictor (kun STRIK ter) — a snake that kills prey by squeezing it so tightly it cannot breathe

prey (PRAY) — an animal that is hunted by another animal for food

reptile (REP tyl) — that group of scaly, cold-blooded animals including snakes, turtles, lizards, the crocodile family, and the tuatara

species (SPEE sheez) — within a group of closely related animals, such as boas, one certain type (*red-tailed* boa)

INDEX

Further Reading

Bargar, S. and Johnson, L. *Boa Constrictors*. Rourke Publishing, 1986
Martin, James. *Boa Constrictors*. Children's Press, 1998
Stone, Lynn M. *Snakes That Squeeze and Snatch*. Rourke Publishing, 2001

Websites To Visit

• www.petsupport.com/reptiles   • www.ceismc.gatech.edu/zooary/reptiles/boa

About The Author

Lynn Stone is the author of over 400 children's books. He is a talented natural history photographer as well. Lynn, a former teacher, travels worldwide to photograph wildlife in their natural habitat.